Hard Work

A Day with Police Officers

By Jan Kottke

McGraw Hill SRA

Columbus, OH

From: A DAY WITH POLICE OFFICERS by Jan Kottke. Copyright © 2000 by Rosen Book Works, Inc.
Photo Credits: Cover, p. 5, 7, 9, 13, 17, 21 by Thaddeus Harden; p. 11 © FPG; p. 15, 19 © Corbis
Contributing Editor: Jennifer Ceaser
Book Design: Michael DeLisio

SRAonline.com

McGraw Hill SRA

Printed in the United States of America.

Send all inquiries to:
SRA/McGraw-Hill
4400 Easton Commons
Columbus, OH 43219-6188

ISBN 978-0-07-612272-1
MHID 0-07-612272-7

10 11 12 13 MER 25 24 23

The McGraw-Hill Companies

Contents

We are **police officers.**

We help people.

We keep people safe.

We start our day at the **police station.**

We find out where we will **patrol** that day.

CRIME
REWARD

I patrol the roads.

I make sure people don't break the **law.**

I have to write a **ticket** if a person drives too fast.

POLICE DEPARTMENT
CITY OF NEW YORK

We patrol on horses.

There's a big **parade** today.

We make sure that people march safely.

I patrol on a boat.

I make sure that everyone is being safe in the water.

POLICE
DEPARTMENT

I patrol on a bike.

I ride my bike through the park.

I make sure everyone in the park is safe.

POLICE
NYPD
FUJI
POLICE

I work in the street.

I use my hands to tell cars when to stop and go.

I make sure people cross the street safely.

POLICE

I patrol with Buster.

Buster is a police dog.

Buster helps me look for **clues.**

Sometimes I stop and talk to people.

They thank me for keeping them safe.

I'm happy to help them.

POLICE
DEPARTMENT
CITY OF NEW YORK

New Words

clues (klooz) things that help police figure out when someone has done something wrong

law (law) a rule that people must follow

parade (puh-**rayd**) a group of people that march together down a street

patrol (puh-**trol**) to keep a place safe

police officers (puh-**leese aw**-fih-sirz) people who make sure others are safe and follow laws

police station (puh-**leese stay**-shen) a place where police officers work

ticket (**tik**-it) something given to a driver who breaks the law

To Find Out More

Books

Officer Brown Keeps Neighborhoods Safe
by Alice K. Flanagan
Children's Press

Officer Buckle and Gloria
by Peggy Rathmann
Putnam Publishing

Police Officers (In My Neighborhood)
by Paulette Bourgeois, Kim Lafave, and Peter Bourgeois
General Distribution Services

Web Site

Super Trooper
HYPERLINK "http://www.users.fast.net/~louis2/index.html"
This site has information about police officers and the equipment they use. It also includes important safety tips.

Index

About the Author
Jan Kottke is the owner/director of several preschools in the Tidewater area of Virginia. A lifelong early education professional, she is completing a phonics reading series for preschoolers.

Reading Consultants
Kris Flynn, Coordinator, Small School District Literacy, The San Diego County Office of Education

Shelly Forys, Certified Reading Recovery Specialist, W.J. Zahnow Elementary School, Waterloo, IL

Peggy McNamara, Professor, Bank Street College of Education, Reading and Literacy Program